GREATER

PARTICIPANT'S GUIDE

DREAM BIGGER.
START SMALLER.
IGNITE GOD'S VISION
FOR YOUR LIFE.

GREATER

STEVEN FURTICK

with ERIC STANFORD

MULTNOMAH
BOOKS

GREATER PARTICIPANT'S GUIDE
PUBLISHED BY MULTNOMAH BOOKS
12265 Oracle Boulevard, Suite 200
Colorado Springs, Colorado 80921

All Scripture quotations are taken from the Holy Bible, New International Version®,
NIV®. Copyright © 1973, 1978, 1984 by Biblica Inc.™ Used by permission of
Zondervan. All rights reserved worldwide. www.zondervan.com.

ISBN 978-1-60142-451-8
ISBN 978-1-60142-452-5 (electronic)

Copyright © 2012 by Steven Furtick

Cover design by Ryan Hollingsworth

Published in the United States by WaterBrook Multnomah, an imprint of the Crown
Publishing Group, a division of Random House Inc., New York.

MULTNOMAH and its mountain colophon are registered trademarks of Random House Inc.

Printed in the United States of America
2013

10 9 8 7 6 5

SPECIAL SALES
Most WaterBrook Multnomah books are available at special quantity discounts when
purchased in bulk by corporations, organizations, and special-interest groups. Custom
imprinting or excerpting can also be done to fit special needs. For information, please
e-mail SpecialMarkets@WaterBrookMultnomah.com or call 1-800-603-7051.

Contents

Welcome

I tell you the truth, anyone who has faith in me
will do what I have been doing. He will do even
greater things than these, because I am going to
the Father.

—JOHN 14:12

For most of us, the experience of our daily lives is a far cry from
the greater works Jesus talked about in John 14:12. We've had
some big dreams about what God might want for our lives. But
so many of us are stuck in the starting blocks. Or are dragging
along at the back of the pack.

We know we were meant for more. Yet we end up settling
for less.

We're frustrated about where we are. But we're confused about how to move forward.

I think we all know instinctively, even if we can't articulate it exactly, that something isn't squaring up. There's a huge gap between what God said in His Word and the results we see in our lives.

I wonder if you can relate.

If so, you need to know that the frustration that's simmering on the back burner right now might boil over one day, and you'll be bitter about the opportunities you missed. Opportunities to be used by God, to touch lives, to get outside yourself and be a part of something greater. I know it's not easy. But don't tell me it's not possible. Jesus Himself said it was.

The fact is, we have the potential to be so much better than we've become, because God is so much greater than we're allowing Him to be through us.

That's why we've developed this *Greater Participant's Guide*. It's a tool for you and a group of others to use in diving deep into the message of *Greater*—not just considering this message on a conceptual level but wrestling with what it means for *you*. Offering discussion questions combined with personal reflection topics and suggested action steps, it's a guidebook to take with you on the way to the greater life.

Here, as in *Greater,* the prophet Elisha shows us the way. Through four key incidents from his life, we'll be learning four key truths that we've got to know if we want to embark on the greater way.

The DVD that goes along with this participant's guide is strategically designed to present the concepts and enhance the content in a multidimensional way. The teaching sessions on the DVD were filmed at the famous Abbey Road Studios in London. Additionally, each session features support footage that was filmed on location where Elisha performed his miracles in the Holy Land. And each video session on the DVD ends with an original worship song written just for that session and performed at Abbey Road.

We pray that these elements will stir your passion and incite your imagination to seek God for greater things. And I hope you'll bring lots of friends, family, and fellow church members with you on the journey.

How to Use
This Guide

The book *Greater* wasn't designed to stand alone. Instead it was intended to serve as just one piece in a whole set of related resources. I didn't want the message to exist merely as a book that people would read and set aside. I prayed that God would use it to spark a movement in the hearts of men and women everywhere, helped along by every format that's appropriate. I'm grateful to God that He's allowed it to happen.

The participant's guide you hold in your hands is an important part of the *Greater* resources. Our vision is that people will use this participant's guide...

- in adult or youth small groups, Bible studies, Sunday school classes, or ministry team meetings

- on a church-wide basis along with a four-week series of sermons
- for leadership training and personal development in business and community settings
- as individuals or couples

However you choose to use this participant's guide, I hope you will maximize your experience by using it in conjunction with the core book, the *Greater* DVD, and the *Greater* collection of worship songs. Also check out the greaterbook.com website for more information and updates.

This participant's guide doesn't simply cover all the same points the book does. Instead it builds on the foundation of the book, offering expanded biblical and practical reflections on the principles in *Greater*. It focuses on four images from the prophet Elisha's life—how he burned his plows, commanded some kings to dig ditches for water, raised a boy from the dead, and struck the waters of the Jordan River with his mentor's cloak. In exploring these four images, it also presents four key ideas that are crucial to pursuing the greater life. Here's how we've broken them down:

 Burn the Plows: To pursue a new life that is greater, we first have to make a decisive break with our old lives. (See also chapter 4 of *Greater*.)

Digging Ditches: We can start small as we seek a greater life, but we need to make practical preparations that demonstrate our faith. (See also chapter 5 of *Greater*.)

 Upon Further Review… We can't let ourselves become discouraged as we advance toward God's greater purpose, because our faith is never wasted. (See also chapter 8 of *Greater*.)

 Strike the Water: For each of us, there comes a time to step out on the word God has spoken to us about a greater life. (See also chapter 12 of *Greater*.)

These are the truths I talk about on the DVD, which includes five video sessions. The first video session is introductory, and I suggest you watch it before the first group session to get an idea of the flow of the study. For example, if you're in an established weekly small group that's going to be using this participant's guide, you could watch the introductory video session as a group the week prior to starting your *Greater* study. The four numbered video sessions go along with the four group sessions, one after the other.

Obviously, many using these resources are already experienced group leaders and have a clear sense of how your meetings should be organized and conducted to fit your context. But for those who want a little more direction, here are some suggestions to get you started.

Group Use

If you're using this participant's guide in a small group of some kind, try to keep the size to no more than a dozen people so that everyone can share easily. You'll need to meet in a place where you can watch a DVD on a large screen and then sit comfortably to discuss the questions. There's enough material for about an hour's worth of meeting time, though you can shrink it or stretch it, if you need to, depending on how your group manages the discussion time.

The Sessions

The sessions are designed to follow a simple format. You'll find an introduction you can read and an opening question that will help to establish how the session topic applies to your life. Then you'll watch the video for that session, taking notes on your own as you watch. Each teaching will conclude with a portion of an original worship song inspired by the message of *Greater*. Hopefully, this will establish an atmosphere for a productive extended time of group discussion that breaks down the key idea for the session and starts to apply it in the participants' lives. Look for the discussion questions in italics. Finally, you'll conclude your time with prayer.

Group Leader

One person should serve as the facilitator of the group sessions. This isn't a formal class, and there's no need for anyone to lecture or dominate the group, but someone should take responsibility for keeping the discussion rolling. See the Leader's Helps at the back of this book for more information.

Community

Make these sessions an opportunity for relationship building. Spend time getting to know each other, encouraging and praying for each other. You might want to serve food. Maybe you'll want to put on some Beatles music when your group is

This icon identifies a quote from one of the video sessions on the *Greater* DVD.

This icon identifies a quote from the book *Greater.*

gathering—if that fits the vibe you're trying to create. Consider sharing contact information and keeping in touch between sessions.

Basically, have fun together. There's nothing like pursuing the greater life in the company of people you know and trust.

After the Session

Each chapter ends with a section called After the Session, which includes reflection questions and action steps you can do at home in your spare time. They're optional, of course, but they're

---

Recommended Reading Schedule for *Greater*

If you haven't already read *Greater,* you should do so as you work your way through these sessions.

- Chapters 1–4: read *before* Session 1.
- Chapters 5–6: read *before* Session 2.
- Chapters 7–8: read *before* Session 3.
- Chapters 9–12: read *before* Session 4.

For a review of all the chapters, see the *Greater* Recap at the end of this participant's guide.

---

also recommended. If you'll give them a try, they will help you further personalize the message of *Greater*. They'll keep the momentum going in the transformational process of believing God for greater things.

SESSION 1

Burn the Plows

This session's key idea: To pursue a new life that is greater, we first have to make a decisive break with our old lives.

Jesus said, "Anyone who has faith in me will do what I have been doing. He will do even greater things than these" (John 14:12). So if God has called all of us to do great things, then why do most people not experience them? If everyone is called to that which is *greater*, why do so many people stay stuck?

Elisha's story suggests it's because too often we pick the wrong place to begin pursuing the greater things God has for us.

One day the senior prophet Elijah, having heard a specific instruction from God, came to Elisha and threw his cloak over the younger man's shoulders. This was a well-understood symbolic act of the day. It simply meant, "I designate Elisha as my successor." The two men were in this prophecy thing together now, and someday, after Elijah was gone, Elisha would take over the top spot in Israel's prophetic corps.

So what happened next? Elisha took off with Elijah on his journeys in representing God to the people, right?

No.

Well, yes. But not at once. Elisha knew there was something else he had to do first, something that would burn his bridges to the past.

And it's this example in Elisha's life that shows us how we can keep from getting stuck before we even set out on our journey to what's greater.

Opening Question

Do you feel as if something is holding you back from pursuing God's design to do something greater in your life? If so, what is holding you back?

Video Viewing

If your group hasn't already watched the introductory video on the *Greater* DVD, watch it now. Then watch Video Session 1. While watching Video Session 1, use the spaces that follow to record key points you hear or thoughts you want to remember.

Your Response to the Video

Elisha's availability to God—and our availability

Steven burning his CD collection

Jesus borrowing Peter's boat

Steven getting a Nintendo when at most he was hoping for an Atari

---

Scripture Passages Mentioned in Video Session 1

- 1 Kings 19:15–21—the call of Elisha
- Romans 11:33–12:2—living sacrifices
- John 14:12—doing greater things than Jesus
- Matthew 14:22–33—Jesus and Peter walking on water
- Ephesians 3:20–21—"immeasurably more"
- Hebrews 3:7–8—hearing God's voice

Having a "ringing in your spiritual ears"

Group Discussion

1. *What challenged you most in Video Session 1, and why?*

The real risk isn't in launching out into a new life of greater things. It's staying in your old life of the ordinary.

2. Read about Elisha's calling to prophetic ministry in 1 Kings 19:19–21:

> *Elijah went from there and found Elisha son of Shaphat. He was plowing with twelve yoke of oxen, and he himself was driving the twelfth pair. Elijah went up to him and threw his cloak around him. Elisha then left his oxen and ran after Elijah. "Let me kiss my father and mother good-by," he said, "and then I will come with you."*
>
> *"Go back," Elijah replied. "What have I done to you?"*
>
> *So Elisha left him and went back. He took his yoke of oxen and slaughtered them. He burned the plowing equipment to cook the meat and gave it to the people, and they ate. Then he set out to follow Elijah and became his attendant.*

In the video Steven talks about Elisha's burning of his plowing equipment—the tools he used in his former career—as being a sign that he was surrendered to God's will and ready to sacrifice his control over his life. He wasn't ever going back to being a farmer.

"Surrender." "Sacrifice." What do you think makes those two words appropriate in describing how we're to be ready to do whatever God asks?

3. *Would you say that, at this point in your life, you are surrendered to God and ready to sacrifice to fulfill His will? Why or why not?*

The first step that Elisha made toward God was not to follow after Elijah, which represented God's purpose for his life, but to burn his plows so he had nothing to go back to.

4. A lot of people don't go after greater things because they think they're no good to start with. What they're forgetting is that none of us does great things for God in our own power. God does great things through us.

Do you struggle with feelings of self-condemnation? If so, where are these feelings coming from? How do they interfere with your obedience to God? How could a clearer understanding of God's greatness help you move toward a sense of affirmation?

Before God can begin to make something greater out of our life, we've got to give all of the life that we have, because He gave it to us to begin with.

5. *What are you worried about losing if you surrender your life to God for His purposes?*

6. Recall Steven's story about the Christmas when he got a Nintendo instead of the Atari he asked for. God may take things away from us, but it's not because He's hateful; it's because He wants to give us something more.

   When has God surprised you by giving you something greater than you expected? Describe the experience.

7. Sometimes God tries to tell us something, but because we have developed a "spiritual ringing of the ears," we don't hear Him.

Considering the questions Steven asked in his "spiritual hearing test," how acute would you say your spiritual hearing is?

___ *Very good*

___ *Good*

___ *Below average*

___ *Practically deaf*

Explain your response.

Because God is so great, He can take someone like me—who apart from Him can do no good—and do greater things through me.

Spiritual Hearing Test

- When was the last time God told you to encourage somebody and you did?
- When was the last time God showed you a trouble spot in a relationship with somebody where you weren't necessarily wrong but you went to that person anyway and tried to make the relationship right?
- When was the last time God showed you something you were doing that wasn't necessarily bad, but wasn't completely what He wanted for your life, and you stopped it just because He said so?
- When was the last time God told you to stop committing a certain sin and you gave it all you had in trying to quit?
- When was the last time God told you to have a hard conversation and you had it?
- When was the last time God told you to take a bold risk for Him and you took the risk?

8. *If our spiritual hearing is not what it could be, how can we go about improving it?*

9. *Are you starting to have a sense yet of what God's greater call might look like in your life? If so, what is it? Where are you in your pursuit of it?*

Before you journey any further into this experience, you need to acknowledge how great God is, how He surpasses everything else in the world you could aim for, and how you'll never be great on your own.

10. Steven says that if you're going to have a greater life, you've got to burn your plow—make a decisive break with whatever's keeping you stuck in your old life. (For examples of the kinds of plows you might have in your life, see page 40 of *Greater*.)

    What plow do you think God is calling you to burn? How do you think burning it will help you pursue the goal of greater things in your life?

11. Sometimes it helps to have a symbolic sign or ceremony to mark a change you're making in your life, like Elisha burning his plow or Steven burning his CD collection. (See pages 46–47 of *Greater* for other examples of ways to break symbolic connections to your present life.)

If you can think of one, what sign or ceremony would help you mark the change you want to make in your life?

Closing Prayer

Spend some time in prayer, offering yourselves to God for Him to use in whatever greater way He wants.

AFTER THE SESSION

Here are a few follow-up activities to help make the key idea of Session 1 more personal to you.

My Time with God

Read Romans 11:33–12:2, a passage that shows how an understanding of God's greatness should lead to sacrifice, transformation, and a renewed ability to say yes to God's will. It starts with a poem of praise and moves on to specific commands. Note how its turning point is marked by a "therefore."

> *Oh, the depth of the riches of the wisdom and knowledge*
> *of God!*
> *How unsearchable his judgments,*
> *and his paths beyond tracing out!*
> *"Who has known the mind of the Lord?*
> *Or who has been his counselor?"*
> *"Who has ever given to God,*
> *that God should repay him?"*
> *For from him and through him and to him are all things.*
> *To him be the glory forever! Amen.*
>
> *Therefore, I urge you, brothers, in view of God's*
> *mercy, to offer your bodies as living sacrifices, holy*

and pleasing to God—this is your spiritual act of worship. Do not conform any longer to the pattern of this world, but be transformed by the renewing of your mind. Then you will be able to test and approve what God's will is—his good, pleasing and perfect will.

Consider these personal reflection questions:

- *What are some of the things—in nature, in art, in history, in Scripture, or in my own relationships or life experience—that remind me of God's magnificent greatness?*
- *How does God's greatness make me feel about Him? What hopes does it give me for myself?*
- *What's keeping me from being totally abandoned to God's purposes in my life right now?*

Spend some unhurried time in prayer, praising God for His greatness, offering yourself to do the greater thing He has in mind for you, and asking Him what He wants you to give up first. Don't do all the talking; remember to listen to Him in silence too.

In the journaling space that follows, record any insights you receive from God:

My Action Step

Before following Elijah as a prophet, Elisha burned the plows that represented his former life in farming. When giving up his rock star aspirations and beginning a new life with church ministry in mind, Steven burned his collection of music CDs. What kind of decisive break do you need to make with your past if you are going to move on to God's greater life for you? And what outward action could serve as a sign to you and to others that you're really making this break?

Plan your own "plow-burning ceremony" below. Think about things like this: What are you going to do? What do you need for it? What's the right time? the right place? Who could you ask to witness or participate?

A plan for my plow-burning ceremony:

SESSION 2

Digging Ditches

This session's key idea: We can start small as we seek a greater life, but we need to make practical preparations that demonstrate our faith.

There are two major reasons why well-intentioned people like us get stuck after we burn our plows.

One, we don't think big enough.

Two, we don't start small enough.

Thinking big enough and starting small enough are two sides of the same coin. So we not only need to dream bigger dreams for our lives, but we also need to take realistic steps of obedience that can actually make God's vision come to life.

In Elisha's day, a combined army under the kings of Israel, Judah, and Edom was stuck, literally. They had gotten as far as a desert when they ran out of water, and the gullies all around them were dry. Meanwhile, their enemies, the Moabites, were massing on the border. What was the allied army going to do about getting water so they could survive and continue their campaign?

The kings called in Elisha, hoping that through him God might signal whether He was going to send some water to get them out of this bind. And as a matter of fact, God did express His intention to send water. But before that happened, the army had some work to do.

Opening Question

When you think about your part in going after greater things, would you say that you...

_____ *are doing everything you possibly can right now?*

_____ *are making an effort but could do more?*

Miracles aren't magic tricks. They are the divine results of small steps of faith-filled preparation.

____ are sitting back and waiting for something to happen without you?

Explain your answer.

Video Viewing

Watch Video Session 2. While watching this video session, use the spaces that follow to record key points you hear or thoughts you want to remember.

Your Response to the Video
Guitar Hero

Elisha telling the kings to dig ditches

Dumb dichotomies

Behind-the-scenes preparation

Digging a ditch today for rain tomorrow

Bench-pressing

Group Discussion

1. *What challenged you most in Video Session 2, and why?*

Scripture Passages Mentioned in Video Session 2
• 2 Kings 3—Elisha and the command to dig ditches
• James 2:14-26—faith without works
• Hebrews 11:1—the nature of faith
• Proverbs 23:7 (KJV) and Luke 6:45—thinking in the heart, speaking from the mouth
• 2 Kings 4:1-7—the widow's oil
• Psalm 119:11—hiding God's Word in the heart

2. Read 2 Kings 3:9–20, the story of Elisha coming to the rescue of three kings and their thirsty army:

> *The king of Israel set out with the king of Judah and the king of Edom. After a roundabout march of seven days, the army had no more water for themselves or for the animals with them.*
>
> *"What!" exclaimed the king of Israel. "Has the LORD called us three kings together only to hand us over to Moab?"*
>
> *But Jehoshaphat asked, "Is there no prophet of the LORD here, that we may inquire of the LORD through him?"*
>
> *An officer of the king of Israel answered, "Elisha son of Shaphat is here. He used to pour water on the hands of Elijah."*
>
> *Jehoshaphat said, "The word of the LORD is with him." So the king of Israel and Jehoshaphat and the king of Edom went down to him.*
>
> *Elisha said to the king of Israel, "What do we have to do with each other? Go to the prophets of your father and the prophets of your mother."*

"No," the king of Israel answered, "because it was the LORD who called us three kings together to hand us over to Moab."

Elisha said, "As surely as the LORD Almighty lives, whom I serve, if I did not have respect for the presence of Jehoshaphat king of Judah, I would not look at you or even notice you. But now bring me a harpist."

While the harpist was playing, the hand of the LORD came upon Elisha and he said, "This is what the LORD says: Make this valley full of ditches. For this is what the LORD says: You will see neither wind nor rain, yet this valley will be filled with water, and you, your cattle and your other animals will drink. This is an easy thing

One reason we feel insecure in our relationship with God is because we're comparing our behind-the-scenes footage to everybody else's highlight reel.

in the eyes of the LORD; he will also hand Moab
over to you. You will overthrow every fortified
city and every major town. You will cut down
every good tree, stop up all the springs, and ruin
every good field with stones."

The next morning, about the time for
offering the sacrifice, there it was—water
flowing from the direction of Edom! And the
land was filled with water.

In introducing this Bible story in the video session, Steven makes a comparison to the video game *Guitar Hero.* He says that everyone wants to be a rock star but nobody wants to learn the chords. In the same way, everybody wants to see God do a miracle in their lives, but few want to do the work to prepare for the miracle.

How have you seen this to be true in your own life or in the lives of others around you?

3. Steven talks about "dumb dichotomies," referring to the way people sometimes assume that two things are in opposition when really they go together. One example of a dumb dichotomy would be to say that since God does greater things through us, we don't have to do anything to help make it happen.

What would look different if you approached your part and God's part in bringing about a greater life not as either/or but as both/and?

It would have been great if all the army had to do was sit around thinking hydration-related thoughts or had a few guided exercises to help them visualize the water. But that's not how God operates.

4. *Name someone you think is a great example of a person willing to do his or her part in God's work. Tell why this person comes to mind for you. Does this example inspire you or dishearten you, and why?*

Three Types of Ditches Mentioned in the Video Session

1. If we want a greater life in our *relationships,* we might need to dig ditches by speaking words of faith and affirmation, both to ourselves and to those around us.

2. If we want a greater life in our *finances,* we might need to dig ditches by paying down our debts.

3. If we want a greater life in our *holiness,* we might need to dig ditches by memorizing Scripture passages that can keep us from sin.

5. One way to dig ditches is to change our words. We can switch from words of condemnation to words of affirmation, from words of hopelessness to words of faith. Changing our words can wind up changing how we think, how we feel, and what we do.

    Give an example you've observed of the power of speaking words of faith over a situation.

6. Another way to dig ditches is to start using our money more wisely. If our path to a greater future is blocked by a hill of debt, we can start shoveling it away a bit at a time.

    How would getting your financial situation in better order position you for greater things?

7. Yet another way to dig ditches is to memorize
   Scripture, hiding God's Word in our hearts.

   *Have you ever tried to memorize verses from the Bible?
   If so, how did it help you?*

8. *What ditches is God calling you to dig? If you're not sure,
   what might help you figure it out?*

9. *Have you already dug any of those ditches? If so, how are you progressing? If not, what's stopping you?*

10. The best way to get over the paralysis that keeps us from acting is to start small.

   What's the very first small step you need to take toward your greater future?

God doesn't call you to have enough faith to finish. He calls you to have enough faith to get started.

11. The ditches we dig are to make room for the water God will send.

    What kinds of new blessings do you think God wants you to make room for in your life?

Closing Prayer

In your group, ask God to forgive you for the ways you have failed to prepare for His work in your lives. Commit before Him to doing your part beginning now.

AFTER THE SESSION

Here are a few follow-up activities to help make the key idea of Session 2 more personal to you.

My Time with God

Read James 2:14–26, which shows that to separate faith and deeds is to create a dumb dichotomy.

> *What good is it, my brothers, if a man claims to have faith but has no deeds? Can such faith save him? Suppose a brother or sister is without clothes and daily food. If one of you says to him, "Go, I wish you well; keep warm and well fed," but does nothing about his physical needs, what good is it? In the same way, faith by itself, if it is not accompanied by action, is dead.*
>
> *But someone will say, "You have faith; I have deeds."*
>
> *Show me your faith without deeds, and I will show you my faith by what I do. You believe that there is one God. Good! Even the demons believe that—and shudder.*
>
> *You foolish man, do you want evidence that faith without deeds is useless? Was not our ancestor Abraham*

considered righteous for what he did when he offered his son Isaac on the altar? You see that his faith and his actions were working together, and his faith was made complete by what he did. And the scripture was fulfilled that says, "Abraham believed God, and it was credited to him as righteousness," and he was called God's friend. You see that a person is justified by what he does and not by faith alone.

In the same way, was not even Rahab the prostitute considered righteous for what she did when she gave lodging to the spies and sent them off in a different direction? As the body without the spirit is dead, so faith without deeds is dead.

Consider these personal reflection questions:

- *How have I separated the things I do from what I believe in my life?*
- *What's keeping me from matching personal action to what I believe? Am I lazy? misguided? Or is there another reason?*
- *What actions do I most need to start doing right now?*

Spend time with God in prayer, confessing the ways you have divorced deeds from faith in your life. Ask Him to show you how you can follow Him more actively.

In the journaling space below, record your thoughts and insights:

My Action Step

In Video Session 2, Steven describes what he calls a "bonus track" idea. He points out that even though God told the army of the three kings to make the valley full of ditches, He sent the water the next day—that is, at a time when they'd just gotten started on the task. In other words, He blessed them immediately after they started small. This goes to show that the simple act of taking a step can be enough to cause God to act in your life.

In the space that follows, list all the ditches you can dig—all the things you can think to do in order to prepare for greater things in your life. (See the examples of small starts for big dreams on page 68 of *Greater*.) Then circle one or more that represent the first steps you can take to pursue your goal.

Then do it.

The ditches I can dig:

SESSION 3

Upon Further Review...

This session's key idea: We can't let ourselves become discouraged as we advance toward God's greater purpose, because our faith is never wasted.

Most of us give up too soon on the greater life God has for us.

The key to perseverance is holding on to the belief that, with God, nothing in your life is ever beyond resuscitation. And even in situations that feel wasted, wrapped in sorrow, or cold to the touch, He has the power to bring forth one thousand new lives.

This is the hope that sustained the faith of a woman who was deeply connected to the prophet Elisha.

For a long time she was childless, and her vision of a greater future included having a son. So through the prophet, God promised her a son—and, as always, He fulfilled His promise. It was a miracle. She was thrilled with the boy she was able to give birth to after thinking there was no chance of ever having him.

Sometime later, though, the boy died. What had happened to God's promise now? She hadn't wanted to have a son for just a few years. She wanted to see him grow up, marry, and have children of his own. She wanted to die knowing that her family would carry on after her. Surely God wouldn't give her this boy for such a short time, only to take him away, would He?

Even with her son lying dead on a couch in her house, she didn't give up. She wouldn't leave Elisha alone until he delivered another miracle.

Opening Question

As you think about moving ahead toward greater things in your life, what's discouraging you right now?

Video Viewing

Watch Video Session 3. While watching this video session, use the spaces that follow to record key points you hear or thoughts you want to remember.

Your Response to the Video

The Shunammite boy's resuscitation

Upon further review...

Abraham's son

Finishing the devil's sermon

Good coming from evil

Even when the worst
thing happens and no
conceivable hope is left,
God still surprises. No
promise from God is
ever completely dead.

Papa's "100 percent"

> ### Scripture Passages Mentioned
> ### in Video Session 3
>
> - 2 Kings 4:8-37—raising the Shunammite's son
> - Romans 4—Abraham's faith
> - John 8:36—free indeed
> - Matthew 4:1-11—the temptation of Jesus
> - 1 John 2:16—cravings, lust of the eyes, boasting
> - Romans 8:37—more than conquerors
> - John 10:10—a thief who comes to kill, steal, and destroy
> - Genesis 50:20—God intended it for good
> - Romans 8:28—working all things for good
> - Numbers 13—Joshua and Caleb's bold report
> - Matthew 18:21-22—forgiving seventy-seven times

Group Discussion

1. *What challenged you most in Video Session 3, and why?*

2. Read 2 Kings 4:8–37, a story of life, death, and seven sneezes:

> *One day Elisha went to Shunem. And a well-to-do woman was there, who urged him to stay for a meal. So whenever he came by, he stopped there to eat. She said to her husband, "I know that this man who often comes our way is a holy man of God. Let's make a small room on the roof and put in it a bed and a table, a chair and a lamp for him. Then he can stay there whenever he comes to us."*
>
> *One day when Elisha came, he went up to*

his room and lay down there. He said to his servant Gehazi, "Call the Shunammite." So he called her, and she stood before him. Elisha said to him, "Tell her, 'You have gone to all this trouble for us. Now what can be done for you? Can we speak on your behalf to the king or the commander of the army?'"

She replied, "I have a home among my own people."

"What can be done for her?" Elisha asked.

Gehazi said, "Well, she has no son and her husband is old."

Then Elisha said, "Call her." So he called

Are you going to believe that the promise of God or the predicament you're in has the final authority in your situation?

her, and she stood in the doorway. "About this time next year," Elisha said, "you will hold a son in your arms."

"No, my lord," she objected. "Don't mislead your servant, O man of God!"

But the woman became pregnant, and the next year about that same time she gave birth to a son, just as Elisha had told her.

The child grew, and one day he went out to his father, who was with the reapers. "My head! My head!" he said to his father.

His father told a servant, "Carry him to his mother." After the servant had lifted him up and carried him to his mother, the boy sat on her lap until noon, and then he died. She went up and laid him on the bed of the man of God, then shut the door and went out.

She called her husband and said, "Please send me one of the servants and a donkey so I can go to the man of God quickly and return."

"Why go to him today?" he asked. "It's not the New Moon or the Sabbath."

"It's all right," she said.

*She saddled the donkey and said to her ser-
vant, "Lead on; don't slow down for me unless I
tell you." So she set out and came to the man of
God at Mount Carmel.*

*When he saw her in the distance, the man
of God said to his servant Gehazi, "Look!
There's the Shunammite! Run to meet her and
ask her, 'Are you all right? Is your husband all
right? Is your child all right?'"*

"Everything is all right," she said.

*When she reached the man of God at the
mountain, she took hold of his feet. Gehazi
came over to push her away, but the man of
God said, "Leave her alone! She is in bitter dis-
tress, but the LORD has hidden it from me and
has not told me why."*

Sometimes in order to believe the
truth about what God has said,
you have to get past the facts and
stand on something more solid.

*"Did I ask you for a son, my lord?" she
said. "Didn't I tell you, 'Don't raise my hopes'?"*

*Elisha said to Gehazi, "Tuck your cloak
into your belt, take my staff in your hand and
run. If you meet anyone, do not greet him, and
if anyone greets you, do not answer. Lay my
staff on the boy's face."*

*But the child's mother said, "As surely as
the LORD lives and as you live, I will not leave
you." So he got up and followed her.*

*Gehazi went on ahead and laid the staff on
the boy's face, but there was no sound or
response. So Gehazi went back to meet Elisha
and told him, "The boy has not awakened."*

When Elisha reached the house, there was

Every dead area of your life is
under further review when you
send it upstairs, to the God who
has a higher vantage point and
sees your situation from angles
you can't access.

the boy lying dead on his couch. He went in, shut the door on the two of them and prayed to the LORD. Then he got on the bed and lay upon the boy, mouth to mouth, eyes to eyes, hands to hands. As he stretched himself out upon him, the boy's body grew warm. Elisha turned away and walked back and forth in the room and then got on the bed and stretched out upon him once more. The boy sneezed seven times and opened his eyes.

Elisha summoned Gehazi and said, "Call the Shunammite." And he did. When she came, he said, "Take your son." She came in, fell at his feet and bowed to the ground. Then she took her son and went out.

A Prayer When Prayers Don't Seem to Be Answered

God, I'm going to have You review this situation. I'm asking You to turn it around. But even if You don't, I'll be grateful because, as I face the facts, I'm determined to keep my faith that nothing is ever wasted.

Steven says that this story is an example of how God is like a football official who reviews a play on the field. When God gives His ruling and overturns the call on the field, suddenly everything is different. (For examples of areas of our lives that might seem dead when they are still alive, see page 117 of *Greater*.)

What circumstance in your life are you hoping that God will reverse upon His further review?

3. *What have been some of the most memorable times in the past when you've experienced God's blessing or goodness in ways you never expected?*

4. *What are one or more areas in your life right now where you feel as if you've wasted your faith and your prayers? How might your faith bear fruit in a way you weren't originally expecting?*

5. Facts are important to take seriously—we need to accept what's really going on. But faith is superior to the facts, because God can always change the facts.

Do you believe that God can bring forth new life even out of the painful deaths you've experienced in your life?

How is your faith contradicting the facts in your life right now?

6. God doesn't always change our circumstances. Sometimes He changes *us*.

   Give an example of a time when you've seen that outcome.

7. At His temptation in the desert, Jesus finished the devil's sermon for him. In other words, each time the devil encouraged Jesus to do something that wasn't a part of His mission, Jesus shot back with a scripture that showed where the devil was wrong.

What sermon is the devil preaching to you right now? How can you rewrite the ending of his sermon by using truths and promises from God?

8. Recall the story Steven told about his grandfather (Papa), who always said he was "100 percent!" The fact is, Papa's circumstances were grim and getting grimmer. But his faith remained at the 100-percent level.

In the light of the obstacles you face right now, what percentage of strength is your faith at?

9. *While you are waiting for God to act, how can you draw near to Him and focus on His faithfulness, thus building up your own faith?*

Your doubt can actually drive you closer to God rather than driving you away from God.

Closing Prayer

Boldly ask God to do miracles in each of your lives. Ask Him to change your circumstances or to change you.

AFTER THE SESSION

Here are a few follow-up activities to help make the key idea of Session 3 more personal to you.

My Time with God

Read Romans 8:28–39. In this passage the apostle Paul eloquently states how our faith is vindicated in spite of every appearance of defeat.

> *We know that in all things God works for the good of those who love him, who have been called according to his purpose. For those God foreknew he also predestined to be conformed to the likeness of his Son, that he might be the firstborn among many brothers. And those he predestined, he also called; those he called, he also justified; those he justified, he also glorified.*
>
> *What, then, shall we say in response to this? If God is for us, who can be against us? He who did not spare his own Son, but gave him up for us all—how will he not also, along with him, graciously give us all things? Who will bring any charge against those whom God has chosen? It is God who justifies. Who is he that condemns? Christ Jesus, who died—more than that, who was raised*

to life—is at the right hand of God and is also interceding for us. Who shall separate us from the love of Christ? Shall trouble or hardship or persecution or famine or nakedness or danger or sword? As it is written:

> *"For your sake we face death all day long;*
>   *we are considered as sheep to be slaughtered."*

No, in all these things we are more than conquerors through him who loved us. For I am convinced that neither death nor life, neither angels nor demons, neither the present nor the future, nor any powers, neither height nor depth, nor anything else in all creation, will be able to separate us from the love of God that is in Christ Jesus our Lord.

Consider these personal reflection questions:

- *If God is working for my good in "all things" in my life, what are some of those things?*
- *What condemnation am I feeling these days? What confidence can I have that I can be free of this condemnation?*
- *How would my life be different if I really comprehended that I am more than a conqueror?*

Praise God for the way He's overcoming evil to bring about His ultimate plan of good. Thank Him that, because of Christ, you are secure in His never-ending love.

Record any thoughts you want to remember:

My Action Step

Review Matthew 4:1–11 below. The underlined words are the devil's "sermon" to Jesus. The **bold words** indicate how Jesus responded to the devil's "sermon."

> Jesus was led by the Spirit into the desert to be tempted by the devil. After fasting forty days and forty nights, he was hungry. The tempter came to him and said, "If you are the Son of God, tell these stones to become bread."
>
> Jesus answered, **"It is written: 'Man does not live on bread alone, but on every word that comes from the mouth of God.'"**

Then the devil took him to the holy city and had him stand on the highest point of the temple. "If you are the Son of God," he said, "throw yourself down. For it is written:

> " 'He will command his angels concerning you,
>   and they will lift you up in their hands,
> so that you will not strike your foot against a stone.' "

Jesus answered him, **"It is also written: 'Do not put the Lord your God to the test.' "**

Again, the devil took him to a very high mountain and showed him all the kingdoms of the world and their splendor. "All this I will give you," he said, "if you will bow down and worship me."

Jesus said to him, **"Away from me, Satan! For it is written: 'Worship the Lord your God, and serve him only.' "**

Then the devil left him, and angels came and attended him.

The devil wanted to "steal and kill and destroy" Jesus's mission—the greater life He had been called to in this world (John 10:10). And the devil wants to steal, kill, and destroy your greater life too.

In the space below, identify what kind of "sermons" the devil tends to preach to you. In other words, what words of discouragement, temptation, or distraction does he plant in your thoughts?

The devil's sermons to me:

Jesus quoted from Deuteronomy and Psalms in His retorts to the devil. In the space that follows, write the responses you can make to the devil's sermons using truths from Scripture. (You may want to use a concordance, topical Bible, or other tool to help you find helpful biblical passages.) For example, if the devil is telling you that you'll never break the addiction you're caught in, you can quote back to Him, "If the Son sets you free, you will be free indeed" (John 8:36).

How I would finish the devil's sermons:

Consider memorizing these Scripture passages you've listed so that you can bring them back to mind when you are tempted again.

SESSION 4

Strike the Water

This session's key idea: For each of us, there comes a time to step out on the word God has spoken to us about a greater life.

You haven't been participating in the *Greater* experience by accident. The hand of God is on you right here, right now, and this is your moment. You and your group have looked at inspiring stories from Elisha, who set out to pursue his greater calling. The guarantee for you is the same: whenever you do what God has called you to do—in any situation, in any given moment— He will do something greater.

This is not a moment to look back over your shoulder and replay the comfortable monotony of life behind the plow. This is not a moment to second-guess your capacity to hear from God. All the stories and miracle narratives have been leading up to this moment, pregnant with sacred expectation.

One day Elisha himself reached a point where he had to make a decision to take action...or not. (See 2 Kings 2.) It happened on the far side of the Jordan River when Elijah was taken up to heaven in a whirlwind. Elisha saw this and cried out, "My father! My father! The chariots and horsemen of Israel!" And then Elisha saw his mentor no more.

Elisha tore his clothes to express his grief at losing Elijah. Next he picked up the cloak that had fallen from Elijah and walked back to the edge of the river.

On the other side, the company of prophets was lined up on the shore, facing him. *Who is this Elisha now?* they must have wondered. *Is he still a student and servant of someone greater, or has he now become greater himself?*

They waited and watched. What would Elisha do?

If Elisha stayed on the other side of the Jordan, if he didn't strike the water and move forward in faith, we wouldn't be studying about him today.

Opening Question

Right now, where are you in pursuing God's greater plan for you?

     ____ *I still don't know what I'm supposed to do.*

     ____ *I'm making preparations, but I'm not ready to make
my move yet.*

     ____ *I started, but then somehow I got stuck.*

     ____ *It's well under way.*

Video Viewing

Watch Video Session 4. While watching this video session, use the spaces that follow to record key points you hear or thoughts you want to remember.

Your Response to the Video

The importance of the strike-the-water moment

Staying close to the Guide

Scripture Passages Mentioned in Video Session 4

- 2 Kings 2:1–18—the spirit of Elijah comes onto Elisha
- 2 Kings 5—Naaman healed in the Jordan
- 2 Kings 6:1–7—the floating ax head
- 2 Kings 6:8–23—a vision of the army of heaven
- 2 Corinthians 3:18—ever-increasing glory
- Psalm 48:12–14—our God forever and ever
- Isaiah 53:6—straying sheep
- Psalm 23—the Lord as a shepherd
- Philippians 1:4–6—faithful to complete the good work
- Jeremiah 1:5—a prophet set apart before he was born

Steven's "directional impairment"

We as sheep and God as Shepherd

Canceling the audition and living out our part

Group Discussion

1. *What challenged you most in Video Session 4, and why?*

2. Read 2 Kings 2:1–15, which records the pivotal
   moment when Elisha began to fulfill his prophetic
   calling on his own:

   > When the LORD was about to take Elijah up
   > to heaven in a whirlwind, Elijah and Elisha
   > were on their way from Gilgal. Elijah said to
   > Elisha, "Stay here; the LORD has sent me to
   > Bethel."
   >
   > But Elisha said, "As surely as the LORD lives
   > and as you live, I will not leave you." So they
   > went down to Bethel.
   >
   > The company of the prophets at Bethel came
   > out to Elisha and asked, "Do you know that the
   > LORD is going to take your master from you
   > today?"
   >
   > "Yes, I know," Elisha replied, "but do not
   > speak of it."
   >
   > Then Elijah said to him, "Stay here, Elisha;
   > the LORD has sent me to Jericho."
   >
   > And he replied, "As surely as the LORD lives
   > and as you live, I will not leave you." So they
   > went to Jericho.
   >
   > The company of the prophets at Jericho

*went up to Elisha and asked him, "Do you know that the L*ORD *is going to take your master from you today?"*

"Yes, I know," he replied, "but do not speak of it."

Then Elijah said to him, "Stay here; the L*ORD has sent me to the Jordan."*

And he replied, "As surely as the L*ORD lives and as you live, I will not leave you." So the two of them walked on.*

Fifty men of the company of the prophets went and stood at a distance, facing the place where Elijah and Elisha had stopped at the Jordan. Elijah took his cloak, rolled it up and struck the water with it. The water divided to

Jesus is the only one who ever arrived and could rightfully say, "It is finished." But for you, it's just beginning.

*the right and to the left, and the two of them
crossed over on dry ground.*

*When they had crossed, Elijah said to Eli-
sha, "Tell me, what can I do for you before I am
taken from you?"*

*"Let me inherit a double portion of your
spirit," Elisha replied.*

*"You have asked a difficult thing," Elijah
said, "yet if you see me when I am taken from
you, it will be yours—otherwise not."*

*As they were walking along and talking
together, suddenly a chariot of fire and horses
of fire appeared and separated the two of
them, and Elijah went up to heaven in a
whirlwind. Elisha saw this and cried out,
"My father! My father! The chariots and
horsemen of Israel!" And Elisha saw him no
more. Then he took hold of his own clothes
and tore them apart.*

*He picked up the cloak that had fallen
from Elijah and went back and stood on the
bank of the Jordan. Then he took the cloak that
had fallen from him and struck the water with
it. "Where now is the LORD, the God of Elijah?" he asked. When he struck the water, it*

divided to the right and to the left, and he
crossed over.

The company of the prophets from Jericho,
who were watching, said, "The spirit of Elijah
is resting on Elisha." And they went to meet him
and bowed to the ground before him.

For Elisha, his time as an apprentice was over. It was time for him to assume leadership of prophecy in Israel. And he displayed his willingness in a dramatic way—by striking the water with his mentor's mantle and causing it to part. After that moment, history would be rewritten.

The same God who brought
you to this point has promised
to be with you to the end and
be your guide. Not just to give
you direction, but to direct you.
Not just to show you His will,
but to show you Himself. Not
just to tell you where to go, but
to empower you to get there.

We all reach the same kind of critical decision point. (To see some examples of areas of life where people can strike the water, review the prayers on pages 186–87 of *Greater*.)

What might your strike-the-water moment look like?

Elijah passed on his mantle to Elisha. Through your surrender to God's Spirit, the mantle of Elisha has been passed on to you.

A Prayer for You

I pray that the same Spirit that raised Jesus Christ from the dead would now come and give life to all of your dead dreams, that you would start small with simple obedience but dream big for the glory of God, and that His vision—His greater vision for your life—would be ignited in a way that would change the world forever.

3. Elisha asked, "Where now is the LORD, the God of Elijah?" (verse 14). Clearly the answer is that the Lord had not retreated to heaven with Elijah but was still present on the earth and was ready to act in and through Elisha.

   Where do you see the Lord at work in your life right now?

4. A group of prophets was watching to see what Elisha would do.

   Who is watching to see what you will do? What is at stake for them in whether you strike the water?

5. The first of two major pieces of advice that Steven gives in this video session is to stay close to our Guide. We need to cultivate our relationship with God so that we can hear His step-by-step instructions.

   How can we stay close to God our Guide?

6. Steven alludes to Isaiah 53:6 in saying that we are like sheep, with a tendency to go our own way.

How are you prone to go astray from the Lord's direction? Identify a recent example.

For everybody who is sick of playing it safe, for every dreamer who has been devastated and disillusioned, for every undiscovered Elisha determined to show a watching world the greater things our God is capable of...your moment is now. The mantle is yours. Nothing is impossible.

7. The second major piece of advice that Steven gives is to cancel the audition and start playing our part. In other words, because God has already called us to a greater life, we can stop trying out for our role and start living up to it.

In what ways have you been preparing for an audition instead of playing your part?

8. According to Jeremiah 1, God told Jeremiah that even before he was born, God had chosen him to be a prophet.

Do you think God chose you for a particular role even before you were born? If so, what do you think that role is?

9. *What remaining fears or questions do you still have about going after greater things? What hopes and expectations do you have?*

10. *What are your plans for pursuing greater things? How can the group help you as you go forward?*

Closing Prayer

Spend time praying together for God to bless you as you strike the water and cross over the Jordan River to the greater life He has for you. Ask Him to use you in a big way to do good in the world and bring glory to Him.

AFTER THE SESSION

Here are a few follow-up activities to help make the key idea of Session 4 more personal to you.

My Time with God

As you're looking at crossing your own Jordan River to a greater life, it's normal to feel some fear or uncertainty. You may be concerned that you'll face struggles. And, in fact, you will. But this is your moment to cross over, and you'll never do it if you stand there paralyzed by the problems you see. You can trust that God will always be there for you and will be faithful to you.

Read Psalm 48:1–8, 12–14:

Great is the LORD, and most worthy of praise,
    in the city of our God, his holy mountain.
It is beautiful in its loftiness,
    the joy of the whole earth.
Like the utmost heights of Zaphon is Mount Zion,
    the city of the Great King.
God is in her citadels;
    he has shown himself to be her fortress.

When the kings joined forces,
    when they advanced together,

they saw her and were astounded;
    they fled in terror.
Trembling seized them there,
    pain like that of a woman in labor.
You destroyed them like ships of Tarshish
    shattered by an east wind.

As we have heard,
    so have we seen
in the city of the LORD Almighty,
    in the city of our God:
    God makes her secure forever....

Walk about Zion, go around her,
    count her towers,
consider well her ramparts,
    view her citadels,
    that you may tell of them to the next generation.
For this God is our God for ever and ever;
    he will be our guide even to the end.

In this psalm God assures the people of Jerusalem that He will be present with them when they face attack. After the battle, they will be able to take a look around their city and see that it is still standing. God will never leave them.

This is the same assurance that *you* can embrace for whatever struggles may lie ahead.

Consider these personal reflection questions:
- *What am I fearful about as I look toward the future?*
- *What do I need God for the most in what lies ahead?*
- *How can I bring my faith into a position of greater prominence than my fear in my daily life?*

Remembering who God is—mighty, loving, faithful—praise Him for the protection He promises. Give Him all your fears and cares. Commit to follow Him into the future that He desires as He leads and accompanies you.

Journal your thoughts here:

My Action Step

Crossing the Jordan River is an act that speaks of change, of leaving one life and entering another. Elisha crossed the literal Jordan River after striking the water with Elijah's cloak. You're crossing a kind of Jordan River too as you begin God's greater life for you.

Of course, you don't know everything that lies ahead. But you know the God who goes before you. And you know something about what He's promised to you.

Prayerfully consider how God wants you to strike the water, to begin your greater life. In the space below, write down what you are going to do.

Striking the water:

On one side of the river below, write things you are leaving behind from your old life. On the other side, write things you believe, in faith, that you are heading toward. Keep this drawing so that you can look back at it in the future as a reminder of what has changed forever.

Leader's Helps

Being the leader of a group using the *Greater Participant's Guide* isn't hard work. It's mainly a process of facilitating the discussion. Yet if you're willing to take on that leadership role, it will give you a chance to help bring about the new life that God is birthing in the group members. So make the most of it.

Thanks for your investment in the greater purpose God is accomplishing in the lives of others.

Tips for the Group Leader:

- Think about how you might want to promote your *Greater* discussion group. For example, do you want to schedule a presentation at your church? Check out the *Greater* DVD for ideas to help you in advertising the group experience. You can also access more of the original worship songs that were recorded as a companion to the *Greater* experience by visiting greaterbook.com. Make sure that everyone who chooses to participate in the group has a copy of *Greater* as well as a copy of this participant's guide. Encourage them to read the first four chapters of *Greater* before coming to the first session. Gather phone numbers or e-mail addresses so that you can communicate with the participants. Give them a reminder of when and where the first session is to be held.

- Each week before your group gets together, watch the video session, read the Bible story from Elisha's life, and work through the participant's guide session on your own. Think through the key points—what they mean to you, what they might mean to your group members. Pray for God to be at work in you and in your group.

- If you're going to have refreshments, arrange for someone to take care of that.

- Get to the group meeting location ahead of time to ensure you have everything you need. Test the video equipment to make sure that it's working and that you know how to play the DVD on it. If you're going to play one of the *Greater* worship songs or other music, make sure equipment is ready for that too. Have some extra

Bibles, plus pens and notepaper on hand. Check to see that the seating, lighting, room temperature, and so on are suitable for a comfortable meeting time.

- Welcome everyone who shows up. Introduce participants to each other if they're not already acquainted. Perhaps you'll want to have an icebreaker question ready at the beginning of at least the first session to help people feel more comfortable with one another.

- Whether at the beginning of a session or at the end, you may choose to take personal prayer requests and lead the group in prayer for them.

- During the discussion time, ask the questions aloud for the group. If some participants seem as though they would like to say more but are feeling too shy for it, gently draw them out. If others are monopolizing the group's time, politely interrupt them and redirect the conversation. Feel free to add to or adapt the questions in the participant's guide to personalize the discussion for your group. Keep watch over the progress of the conversation to make sure you can cover all the important points in the time you have available. Yet if it seems that God is doing something special in the group or in the life of one of the participants, by all means, go with that even if it means deviating from your original plan.

- Encourage group members to use the After the Session sections on their own at home, and participate along with them. You may wish to check in with them on their action steps.
- At your final session, invite your group to go to the greaterbook.com website and share stories of what God is doing in them and through them.

Greater Recap

If you think you could use a review of the book *Greater,* check out this chapter-by-chapter summary of its key points.

Chapter 1. Steve and Me

⮂ RT "Most believers aren't in imminent danger of ruining their lives. They're facing a danger that's far greater: wasting them."

When Apple founder Steve Jobs died, Steven Furtick got to thinking about what constitutes a great life and how one achieves it. He turned to John 14:12, where Jesus says that anyone who has faith in Him will do greater things than He did. Why, Steven wondered, are so many Christians *not* doing great things?

Most people, he observed, are stuck in mediocrity. They may have some grandiose ideas about achieving greatness, but they're not achieving it. Yet there's a third way between the *good enough* that leaves you stuck in stagnation and the grasping for *greatness* that leads to endless frustration. This third way he calls *greater*. He defines it as "the life-altering understanding that God is ready to accomplish a kind of greatness in your life that is entirely out of human reach...but exactly what God has seen in you all along." This kind of greater life is available to all people through believing in Jesus and taking practical steps to get there.

Chapter 2. Lesser Loser Life

RT "In spite of all the parts of us that are anything but good, God is holding the door open to a life that is greater."

Against his desire to lead a greater life, Steven feels the pull toward what he calls his "lesser loser life." This is the tendency to see himself as not good enough or worthy enough to do something great. Even though he's leading a growing church that God is blessing in an amazing way, he still has moments when he recalls his small-town beginnings and thinks, *I don't belong here.*

Most people deal with similar kinds of self-doubt and self-accusation. And the devil likes it that way, because it leaves us stuck and keeps us from accomplishing great things for God. What we need to realize is that doing something greater isn't about what *we* can achieve on our own but about what God can achieve *through us.*

Despite our limitations and past failures, all of us have a potential for greater things. We all need to leave our own lesser loser lives behind and move into the greater life God has for us. The example of the Old Testament prophet Elisha will show us how.

Chapter 3. Dragging Behind

RT "God communicates vision differently to everyone He calls. He is working behind the scenes, orchestrating His destiny for you."

Before he started following the older prophet Elijah, Elisha was a farmer who got up day after day and did the usual kinds of farm work. His pattern at that time was much like the monotonous routines so many of us are trapped in.

But God was up to something in Elisha's life even before he was aware of it. God instructed Elijah to tap Elisha to be his successor as the nation's leading prophet.

God is up to something in our lives too. That's why we have

to stay alert for His presence—so that we are ready to listen when He speaks and to respond when He acts. In the midst of the ordinary, we have to stay faithful while God is working behind the scenes to call us to the extraordinary.

When Elijah placed his mantle on Elisha's shoulders, symbolizing that he was calling Elisha to take over his position, Elisha was ready. He didn't hesitate. He took off running.

Chapter 4. Burn the Plows

RT "When God is speaking, one word is more than enough. He's more interested in your full obedience than your total understanding."

But *before* Elisha took off running after Elijah, there was one thing he wanted to do first. He burned his plowing equipment and used the fire to cook his own oxen. This wasn't just about staging an impromptu feast for his friends. He was making a decisive break with his past.

All of us have things that keep us tied to our old lives. We need to surrender these to God.

Of course, doing so can be scary. When we surrender ourselves to follow God's call to a greater life, He doesn't tell us in detail what to expect. He leads us step by step. Like Abraham moving from Ur when God said, "Go," or like Peter stepping onto the waves when Jesus said, "Come," we have to be ready to obey God's commands without knowing what will come next.

To signal our willingness to follow where God leads us, we need to give up whatever holds us to an earlier way of life. That's what Steven did as a teenager when he chose to burn his collection of CDs.

Giving things up seems costly. But even more costly would be choosing to stay stuck in the old life of the ordinary. And just as Elisha received a double portion of Elijah's anointing, so—if we follow God in faith—the rewards for us will be immense. The whole world will open up for us in a different way.

Chapter 5. Digging Ditches

RT "God will often launch a vision that is larger than life by bringing you to a starting point that is small and seemingly insignificant."

There are two parts to living a greater life. First, you have to think big. Second, you have to start small.

This is what faith is—it's action. You can't just imagine doing greater things. You have to pursue those things with practical steps.

Elisha understood this truth. When an alliance of three kings who had run out of water for their army asked Elisha what to do, he told them to dig ditches to hold the coming water. They did what he told them, taking care of the practical preparation. And so when the water came the next day, they were ready for it.

Only God can bring about miracles in our lives. But He calls us to do our part in getting ready for them. We've all got ditches to dig.

Chapter 6. A Little Oil

🔁 RT "Stop waiting for what you want, and start working what you've got. Your greatest limitation is God's greatest opportunity."

The greater life will look different for different people. It won't always involve a dramatic change or be highly visible so that it is applauded by others. But whatever God calls us to do, it's great in its own way.

The path to the greater life starts with where we are and with what we've got.

Elisha saved a widow from starvation by instructing her to pour out what little oil she had left. God multiplied the oil until this woman had enough to sell to others and sustain her family. In the same way, instead of wishing we had something we don't, we should use whatever we do have for the Lord. He'll multiply and use it.

Chapter 7. Wasted Faith

⟳ RT "The journey toward greater things is marked with set-backs and real suffering. But God has never wasted an ounce of your faith."

The journey toward greater things is rarely straight or smooth. This is true in our lives, and it was true in the experience of Elisha.

The prophet conveyed God's assurance to a childless Shunammite woman that she was finally going to have the son she longed for. And it happened. But a few years later the boy died. What was going on here? God's promises seemed hollow. The mother's path to the greater future she hoped for seemed to have reached a dead end.

When something like this happens to us along our path toward what we think is our greater future, it can seem as if our faith has been wasted. In fact, though, our faith is never wasted.

Chapter 8. Trust Fund Baby

⟳ RT "In God's economy, our greatest setbacks in life can be the greatest setups to seeing God's glory in places we didn't even know to look."

To use an analogy, God has a trust fund where he stores up all the faith we deposit and disburses the proceeds to us in the ways He knows are best. In other words, our prayers are never in vain, even if we don't get what we ask for. God gives us what we need in a greater way than we knew to ask for.

When the Shunammite woman's son died, she didn't give up. And neither did Elisha. The Lord used Elisha to bring the child back to life.

The truth is, when the worst thing has happened and no conceivable hope is left, God still surprises. No promise from God is ever completely dead.

In football an official sometimes reverses the call on the field. Likewise, God reverses the apparently hopeless situations we face on our way toward greater service to Him.

We must never give up hope. We can always draw nearer to God and keep on trusting in Him.

Chapter 9. Saving Captain Awesomesauce

🔁 RT "It's possible to have all the external signs of greatness and yet internally yearn for something greater."

If we start getting proud and thinking we're great on our own merits, we only have to look at Jesus to be put in our place. Any perceived greatness in ourselves shrinks in comparison to who He is. The fact is, without grace we're nothing.

In Elisha's day, the Syrian general Naaman needed to learn such a lesson in humility. Having come to Elisha in hopes of a cure for his leprosy, he was indignant when the prophet sent word that he was to wash in the Jordan River. This treatment seemed beneath him. Yet when he eventually humbled himself enough to follow the instructions, he was healed.

Steven went through a humbling process of his own when he undertook a forty-day fast. Honestly, he hated it. But it helped to deliver him from some of his Naaman-like tendencies.

We all need to humble ourselves. Even Jesus humbled Himself by coming to earth as a man. Becoming greater is never about *our* comfort and *our* glory but about God's glory. We can move toward greater humility by immediately obeying God's specific instructions to us and by keeping ourselves small through our daily interactions with the people around us.

Taking the lowest place brings us the highest power.

Chapter 10. Where Did It Fall?

RT "Greater isn't an automatic, permanent position; it's an intentional daily decision."

For all of us who are following God into the greater life, a moment will come when we lose our spiritual momentum and begin to backslide into the realm of the ordinary. When that happens, we may be tempted to give up. But instead we need to go back to where we lost our edge and get it back.

In Elisha's day, a younger prophet had lost his edge, literally. He had dropped his ax head into the Jordan River. Elisha asked him where it had fallen, and then the two of them went to that spot, where Elisha caused the ax head to float to the surface.

We, too, need to rely on the power of God to restore our spiritual momentum. We need to identify where we got off track, pray about it, and get moving again.

Steven used a Christian counselor to provide preventive counseling designed to help him keep on track as a Christian leader. All of us need to do whatever we have to in order to keep or to get back our spiritual edge.

Chapter 11. Open My Eyes

RT "What matters most is not what you think you are or are not. What matters is what your Father sees in you and what He says about you."

In our pursuit of a greater dream, we're going to come up against enemies who want to hinder us. Many people will criticize, belittle, or oppose what we're trying to do. That's why sometimes we need to put people out of our lives for a season or even forever.

In addition to negative people, we also face an army of distractions and competing ideas, values, interests, and events. Standing behind all these and orchestrating them in opposition to us is our ultimate adversary: Satan.

The key to victory against our enemies is realizing that we're not alone in our battles. God is present with us...if we will only see it.

During the runup to war between Judah and one of its neighbors, an attendant of Elisha became seized with fear as he caught sight of the enemy army. Elisha prayed for God to open this man's eyes to the spiritual reality. God did—and there was the army of heaven all around to protect Judah's forces. The balance of power was decidedly with God's people, not against them.

All of us need to recognize the reality of the might of God in us and around us. We need to believe what our heavenly Father says about us, not what our opponents say about us. If we'll see with the eyes of our hearts, we'll realize that God's power makes us fully capable of accomplishing whatever He calls us to do.

Chapter 12. Strike the Water

RT "For everybody who is sick of playing it safe, for every dreamer who has been disillusioned, your moment is now. The mantle is yours."

The time came when God took the great prophet Elijah up to heaven in a whirlwind. And Elisha was left standing there by himself. A group of prophets was standing on the opposite side of the Jordan River, watching. Did this startling event mean that the power of God had gone away with Elijah? Or did it now reside in Elijah's successor, Elisha?

Elisha took up Elijah's mantle, rolled it up, and struck the surface of the Jordan with it. The water parted so that Elisha could cross on dry ground. And so the prophets' questions were answered. Elisha was filled with God's power, and he had a career of great and mighty deeds ahead of him.

But it took that striking of the water to give a start to Elisha's solo ministry as a prophet.

On our journey to the greater life, we, too, come to a moment when we have to begin. When we have to act. When we have to strike the water.

That moment is now.

About the Author

Steven Furtick, author of the best-selling *Sun Stand Still*, is founder and lead pastor of Elevation Church, which in only six years has grown to more than ten thousand in regular attendance at six locations. He holds a master of divinity degree from Southern Baptist Theological Seminary. He and his wife, Holly, have three children: Elijah, Graham, and Abbey. They make their home near Charlotte, North Carolina.

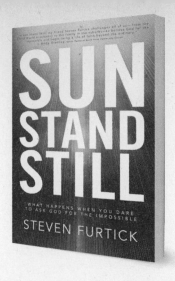

WHAT HAPPENS WHEN YOU DARE TO ASK GOD FOR THE IMPOSSIBLE

If the size of your vision for your life isn't intimidating to you, there's a good chance it is insulting to God.

In his first book, Pastor Steven Furtick challenges you to walk in audacious faith and watch God do the impossible in your life. No dream is too big when God is involved, and there is unlimited potential in the life of every believer through Jesus. Steven shows that faith is the most vital building block in your relationship with God as you live out what He has put in your heart.

IN SUN STAND STILL, YOU WILL DISCOVER HOW TO:

Reconnect with your God-sized purpose and potential

Believe in the promises of God even in uncertainty

Activate your faith through hearing, speaking, and doing the Word of God

Pray with urgency, boldness, and expectancy

Start a movement in your life, your church and your community

FIND OUT MORE ABOUT THE MOVEMENT AT WWW.SUNSTANDSTILL.ORG

GREATER is much more than a book. It is an immersive experience. The new album from Elevation Worship, **NOTHING IS WASTED**, is designed to follow the narrative of **GREATER**. The 12 original songs written by the worship team at Elevation Church correspond with the chapters of the book.

SONGS INCLUDE:

Great In Us

Let Go

In Your Presence

I Have Decided

We're Not Alone

I Will Trust In You

Unchanging God

Nothing Is Wasted

Be Lifted High

Lift Us Out

Open Up Our Eyes

Greater

FOR MORE INFORMATION, VISIT:

WWW.ELEVATIONWORSHIP.COM